S. P. Aggy first became aware of animal welfare in 1999, approximately 6 months after adopting 3 kittens. She began living a lifestyle that reflected this awareness and, over the years, animal welfare has become a passion of hers.

Her hope in writing this book is to gently encourage change in favour of animal welfare.

This collection of poems and facts has been written for the younger generations, but S.P. Aggy hopes that everyone will enjoy them and that maybe a small change will trigger within someone to the benefit of all life.

Illustrations and book design by Lakshmi Skala.

My world too

For Dad – for his unlimited understanding, kindness and unconditional love. We will always love you.

For all the animals in the world

Contents page

Ant... 7

Bear.. 9

Camel... 11

Dog.. 13

Elephant... 15

Flamingo.. 17

Goat.. 19

Hippo.. 21

Iguana... 23

Jaguar... 25

Kangaroo... 27

Lion... 29

Meerkat... 31

Nightingale.. 33

Octopus.. 35

Platypus.. 37

Quetzal... 39

Rhino.. 41

Seahorse... 43

Tortoise.. 45

Umbrellabird... 47

Vole.. 49

Wolf... 51

Xerus.. 53

Yak... 55

Zebra.. 57

Ant

Did you know?

- There are over 12,000 different types (species) of ant in the world
- It is thought there are about 10 quadrillion (10,000,000,000,000,000) ants on the planet

- Ants have been around for about 110 to 130 million years
- Ants live in groups called colonies

- Colonies can be very small and have only a few ants or they can be very big and have millions of ants
- Each ant colony has its own special smell

- Different ants have different jobs to do in their colonies; they can be queens or soldiers or builders or look after the babies and eggs or gather food for the colony
- Ants help and support each other and are known for their excellent teamwork

- Ants are thought to be among the smartest of insects, along with bees
- Apart from people, ants are the only other creatures on Earth who "farm" other animals - ants farm aphids like people farm cows and sheep

- Ants are very strong and can lift between 20 and 100 times their own body weight
- Ants don't have ears; they "listen" through their feet using vibrations in the ground

- Ants don't have lungs and breathe through tiny holes in their bodies
- Ants have 2 sets of jaws
- Most ants can survive a whole day under water

A

"Hello, hello, how do you do?

Good Afternoon, good day to you!

Oh my! Oh my! These ants to greet

So many, so many under my feet!"

Bear

Did you know?

- There are 8 different types (species) of bear in the world - some black, some brown and some white
- Polar bears and some types of brown bear are among the biggest and most powerful land animals in the world

- Bears have such a powerful bite that they can crush a bowling ball
- Bears are shy animals and like to be alone

- Bears are very intelligent - they have big brains, extremely good memories and a better sense of direction than most people
- Bears are fantastic swimmers; most bears can swim up to 6mph and polar bears can easily swim over 60 miles in one go

- Bears are excellent climbers; they can climb up and back down a tree in only a few seconds
- Bears are bowlegged, which helps them to balance when they're standing

- Bears can run really fast - up to 40mph - for short periods of time
- Bears have 2 layers of fur – a short layer underneath to keep them warm and a longer layer on top to keep them dry

- Unlike most other mammals, bears can see in colour
- Bears have an excellent sense of smell, possibly the best sense of smell of any animal on Earth
- Under their white fur polar bears have black skin, and their fur is not actually white - it's see-through

B

Lightning fast and quick as can be

The bear ran up the towering tree

"Did you see that? Did you see!"

The whistling wind chuckled with glee.

Camel

Did you know?

- There are 3 different types (species) of camel in the world - the Dromedary and 2 types of Bactrian
- The Dromedary camel has 1 hump and the Bactrian camel has 2

- Camels' humps don't store water - they store fat which can be used as food in emergencies
- A baby camel is born without a hump but starts growing one as soon as it can eat solid food

- Camels can reach up to 7 feet in height at the hump
- Camels live mainly in deserts where it is very hot and dry and need to find ways of losing as little water as possible from their bodies; they do this by not sweating and having very dry poos

- Camels are often used for carrying people and things and are known as "ships of the desert"
- Camels can survive without food and water for weeks, sometimes even months, and when they do find water, they can drink up to 40 gallons in one go

- Mother camels and baby camels hum to each other
- Camels have 2 sets of eyelids with eyelashes to keep sand out of their eyes, and a third clear eyelid to clean their eyes

- Camels can completely close their noses during a sandstorm
- Camels walk in a different way to other mammals – they move both back and front legs on the same side at the same time so look like they are swaying from side to side

- Camels can run as fast as 40mph
- Camels are known to be very peaceful, social animals unless they are frightened or angry when they will spit aggressively

"Dear Camel, in the desert hot

How many humps have you truly got?"

"I'll tell you, dear child, but only you

I have one, my cousin has two."

Dog

Did you know?

- There are believed to be up to 340 different kinds (breeds) of dog in the world
- Some people think dogs have a sense of time and miss you when you're gone

- Dogs are often called "Man's best friend"
- Dogs can smell people's feelings

- Dogs are as smart as a 2 to 3-year-old child and can understand up to about 250 words
- Dogs have a sense of smell that's more than 10,000 times stronger than people's

- Dogs can hear 4 times further than people, and know where a sound came from within seconds
- A dog's whiskers help it to "see" things in the dark by picking up tiny movements in the air

- Touch is the first sense a dog develops
- Like people's fingerprints, dog nose prints are unique and can be used to identify a dog

- Dogs only sweat from their paws and have to pant to cool themselves down
- Dogs have 3 eyelids

- Dogs have more than 12 separate muscles to control their ears
- A dog's shoulders are not fully connected to the rest of its skeleton and are often called "floating shoulders"

- Dogs can be right-pawed or left-pawed, like people can be right-handed or left-handed
- There is one type of dog in the world, called the Basenji, which can't bark but yodels instead

Deep brown eyes so happy to see me

"I love you," they say longingly

A dog's tail wagging to and fro

"Stay with me, oh please don't go."

Elephant
Did you know?

- There are 3 different types (species) of elephant in the world – the Asian and 2 types of African
- African elephants are the largest and heaviest land animals in the world

- Elephants have the largest brains of land animals, about 3 to 4 times larger than a person's brain, but it is small compared to their big bodies
- Elephants are known to be very kind, caring, sensitive and intelligent animals

- Elephants form very strong family bonds
- The elephant's trunk is actually a long nose used for breathing, smelling, drinking, picking things up, trumpeting and snorkelling

- An elephant's trunk is so strong that it can break a branch from a tree, but also so delicate it can pick up a single blade of grass
- An elephant's trunk has about 100,000 muscles

- Baby elephants suck their trunks for comfort, like some children suck their thumbs
- Elephants have very thick skin - over an inch thick - but it is very sensitive to the touch

- Despite having such big feet, elephants actually walk on their toes
- As well as being known to trumpet, elephants also purr

- Elephants are terrified of bees and will run if they hear a bee swarm
- African elephants can "hear" through their feet
- Though elephants are so large, it is thought their closest relative is a small furry rat-like mammal called the rock hyrax

E

"Dear Elephant, majestic and kind

Gentle giant with a clever mind

Amazing trunk, fantastic feature

You truly are a splendid creature!"

Flamingo

Did you know?

- There are 6 different types (species) of flamingo in the world
- Flamingos are water birds and live in salty lakes and lagoons

- Flamingos are known for standing on one leg for hours with the other leg tucked under their bodies
- Flamingos can stand on one leg so comfortably that they can sleep in that position

- Flamingos are pink because of the food they eat (shrimp & algae). If they stop eating this food, their feathers will turn white
- The flamingos with the pinkest feathers have the highest status in the group

- The feathers under a flamingo's wings are black and can only be seen when the flamingo is flying
- Baby flamingos are grey or white and turn pink in the first few years of their lives

- Flamingos prefer to bend their necks to the right when they rest them on their backs to sleep
- Flamingos have to take a short run to take off into the air to fly but are powerful fliers

- Flamingos eat by tipping their heads upside-down into water, slurping up lots of it and filtering it for food
- Flamingos' nests are tall mounds made from mud, stones, straw and feathers, and are built on the ground

- Flamingos are among the longest living of birds, some even living as long as 70 years
- Flamingos are very social animals; they gather in large flocks and do everything together, like sleeping and eating together

On a bright warm sunny day

The salty lake was heard to say

"Flamingo, stood on one leg so

Where, oh where, did your other leg go?"

Goat

Did you know?

- There are believed to be about 240 different kinds (breeds) of goat in the world
- There are 2 main types of goats - domestic and mountain goats

- Goats are very intelligent and curious animals
- Goats can be taught their name and to come when called, just like dogs

- Both male and female goats can have beards and horns
- Baby goats are called kids; each kid has its own special call and smell which is how its mother recognises it

- Goats are very good climbers and can climb to the tops of trees
- Goats have such good balance that they can easily stand on the tops of trees and the sides of steep mountains

- The pupils in a goat's eyes are a rectangle shape which allows the goat to see all the way round except what's directly behind it
- Goats are very fussy eaters and will only eat clean food; they won't eat hay that's been walked on or left lying around

- Goats burp often and loudly
- Goats don't have upper front teeth or tear ducts

- Goats like to be with other goats in a herd and can become lonely and depressed if kept alone
- Goats were one of the first animals to be tamed by people
- One type of goat, known as the "fainting goat", looks like it's fainted but is actually falling over because its muscles have frozen when it gets excited or frightened

G

The goat climbed to the top of the tree

Curious to see what he could see

He looked around and burped so loud

Then giggled and giggled, oh so proud!

Hippo

Did you know?

- There are 2 different types (species) of hippo in the world – the Common and the Pygmy
- Hippos are only found in Africa, and are the third largest land animal after the elephant and white rhino

- Hippos are thought to be one of the most aggressive animals in the world, and the most dangerous animals in Africa
- Hippos sweat a red substance which looks like blood but is actually a thick red oil that acts as a sunblock, and also helps to keep the hippo's skin moist

- If a hippo's skin dries out, it will crack
- Hippos spend most of the day in water or rolling in mud to keep cool, and will only come out when the sun goes down to go looking for food

- A hippo's eyes, ears and nose are high up on the roof of its skull so it can still see, hear and breathe when the rest of its body is in the water
- Hippos can completely close their ears and noses when they go underwater

- Hippos can't float or swim so stand or walk on the ground underwater
- When hippos are underwater, they have to come back up every 3 to 5 minutes to breathe, and they do this so automatically that a hippo sleeping underwater does it without waking up

- Hippos can run almost as fast as 25mph
- Hippos can open their mouths almost 180 degrees wide

- A hippo's canine teeth can grow up to just over 19 inches long
- A hippo's closest living relatives are whales, dolphins and porpoises

"Hippo oh hippo, rolling in mud

Are you, my goodness, sweating red blood?"

"No, no, dear child, no blood here, no none

I'm sweating red oil to keep off the sun."

Iguana

Did you know?

- It is thought there are between 35 and 44 different types (species) of iguana in the world
- Iguanas live in South and Central America, Mexico, the Caribbean and the Galapagos Islands

- Iguanas are very big lizards that can grow to between 5 and 7 feet long, but more than half of their length is their tail
- Iguanas are among the largest lizards in the Americas

- You can easily recognise an iguana by the saggy skin around its throat and the spines on its head, back and tail
- Iguanas use their tails to defend themselves and can break part of it off to escape if they need to; it will eventually grow back as good as new

- Iguanas have a "third eye" on top of their heads which can't see anything except brightness but is important in letting the iguana know about anything dangerous overhead
- Iguanas are cold-blooded animals and love to spend their days just lazing in the sun to keep warm

- If the weather gets too cold (less than about 4 degrees C) an iguana's muscles become frozen and it falls asleep; it will wake up again when the weather warms up
- Iguanas are very tough creatures; they can fall from very high places, about 40 or 50 feet high, and survive without injury

- Iguanas can hold their breath underwater for up to 30 minutes
- Some iguanas can blow themselves up with air (inflate) so they can float
- Iguanas are social animals and like to live together and eat together

I

"Where's your tail, where has it gone?

What, oh, what is going on?

Iguana there, please tell me so

Where oh, where oh, did it go?"

Jaguar

Did you know?

- There is only one type (species) of jaguar in the world
- Jaguars are only found in the Americas

- Jaguars are the third largest cat in the world after the lion and tiger, and the largest cat in the Americas
- Jaguars prefer to live mainly in forests but can also be found in grasslands and wetlands

- A jaguar's jaws are stronger than any other type (species) of cat, and its bite is so powerful that it can crunch straight through a skull
- A jaguar's spots are unlike any other cat spots; each spot looks like a rose and is called a rosette

- Though jaguars and leopards look similar, jaguars are larger and their spots are bigger with small dots in the middle which leopards don't have
- Black panthers are actually jaguars or leopards but are totally black

- Jaguars are not social animals and prefer to be alone
- Jaguars love the water; they are good swimmers and will often play and bathe in the water

- Jaguars like to hunt for fish and will sometimes do so by using their tails like a fishing line
- Jaguars can run faster than 64mph for a short time

- Jaguars are excellent climbers and can climb trees very easily
- There is a car named after the jaguar

J

See the jaguar, jaws so strong

There he goes, skulking along

Playing in water, catching fish

Time for lunch, a tasty dish!

Kangaroo

Did you know?

- There are 4 different types (species) of kangaroo
- Kangaroos only live in Australia, Tasmania and New Guinea

- Kangaroos are the only large animals that move by hopping
- Kangaroos' back legs are so strong and powerful that they can jump 3 times as high as their own height

- Kangaroos use their tails for balancing while hopping, and if you lift a kangaroo's tail off the ground it can't hop
- Kangaroos can't walk backwards

- Kangaroos are very good swimmers
- Kangaroos can't move their back legs separately from each other on land, only when they are swimming

- Female kangaroos have pouches in the fronts of their bodies in which they carry their babies
- When a baby kangaroo is born it is about the size of a rice grain and immediately crawls into its mother's pouch to continue to grow, and to feed

- Baby kangaroos live in their mothers' pouches for about 8 to 11 months before they are ready to leave
- Kangaroos have excellent hearing and can move their ears in all directions

- Kangaroos are left-handed
- Kangaroos are very social animals and prefer to live in groups
- Kangaroos can survive without drinking any water for months

The wind peered in the kangaroo's pouch

Curious to see, curious to vouch

Was it empty, was it bare?

Or was there really a baby there?

Lion

Did you know?

- There are 2 different types (species) of lion in the world - Asian and African
- Lions are the second largest cat in the world after the tiger

- Though lions are known as "kings of the jungle", they don't live in the jungle; they live in grasslands and plains
- Male lions are easy to recognise because of their big thick manes

- Lions with darker manes are stronger and healthier than lions with lighter coloured manes
- Mane colour can change depending on the lion's health

- Female lions do most of the hunting
- Lions are the most social of the big cats and are the only large cats that like to live in groups

- Lions can spend up to about 20 hours a day just resting and sleeping
- The lion's roar is the loudest of the big cats and can be heard from 5 miles away

- Lions can't roar until they are about 2 years old
- A lion's pupils are 3 times as big as a person's

- Lions are the only cats with tufts at the end of their tails
- A lion's tongue is so rough that if it licked a person's hand a few times it would peel away the skin
- The pattern made by the black spots on the lion's face at the end of its whiskers is unique to each lion

L

The reeds smiled as they watched the birds soar

Frightened by the king's magnificent roar

See the lion with his beautiful mane

Standing so fierce on the grassy plain.

Meerkat

Did you know?

- Meerkats are a type (species) of mongoose
- Meerkats live mainly in the deserts of Africa

- Meerkats like to live together in large groups, called mobs, in underground burrows
- Meerkats are very social animals and like to play with, and groom, each other

- Meerkats recognise each other's voices
- Meerkats heap on top of each other when they go to sleep, snuggling up to each other

- Meerkats often stand upright on their back legs to look around them, using their tails to balance
- Meerkats work very well together as a team; each member of the team is given a different job to do like babysitting, hunting or guarding

- The job of guarding is one of the more important roles and all the meerkats get a chance to be guard
- If the meerkat on guard spots danger it barks loudly or whistles to let the others know to quickly run away and hide in their burrows

- All the meerkats in the mob help to raise all the babies in the mob and teach them important things like what to eat and where to find food
- Meerkats are so scared of birds of prey that a young meerkat will run for cover if it sees a plane

- Meerkats keep warm by standing or lying with their bellies towards the sun
- Meerkats are excellent diggers; they can dig as much dirt as their own body weight in a few seconds
- Meerkats are immune to snake and scorpion poison

Ssh! Be quiet and don't be so loud

The meerkat's standing up in the crowd

He's keeping guard and looking around

A noise, dear child, will send him to ground.

Nightingale

Did you know?

- The nightingale is a small type (species) of bird
- Both male and female nightingales look similar

- Nightingales are generally thought to be quite plain-looking birds but have beautiful singing voices and are possibly the best singers of all birds
- Nightingales' singing is thought to be so beautiful that there are famous poems written about it

- Radio broadcasts of a nightingale singing along to a cello in 1924 were listened to by thousands of people
- Only the male nightingale sings

- Nightingales sing mostly at dawn and dusk but also sing at night sometimes
- When a nightingale sings at night it is usually trying to attract a female nightingale

- Nightingales are shy birds who like to hide so are hard to spot but can easily be heard when singing
- The part of the brain that helps to make sound is bigger in nightingales than in most other birds

- Nightingales don't nest in trees, they build their nests on or just above the ground in dense bushes
- Nightingales live mainly in Europe and Asia but every winter migrate thousands of miles to Africa for the warmer weather

N

The nightingale is a shy little bird

He can't be seen but can be heard

With the sweetest voice he sings his song

Hoping his sweetheart will come along.

Octopus

Did you know?

- There are about 300 different types (species) of octopus, living in seas and oceans all over the world
- Octopuses can be different sizes, ranging from very small (smaller than an inch) to very large (just under 10 feet)

- Octopuses are invertebrates which means they have no bones so their bodies are completely soft
- The only hard part of an octopus is a sharp beak on the underneath of its body

- Octopuses are thought to be the cleverest of all invertebrate creatures
- Octopuses can learn how to do new things from watching other octopuses

- Octopuses prefer to walk along the ocean floor rather than swim but can be fast swimmers if they need to be
- Octopuses don't have "tentacles", they have "arms"

- Two-thirds of an octopus' brain cells are in its arms
- If an octopus loses an arm, it grows back

- Octopuses can squirt a dark ink to confuse or blind an attacker to give themselves time to get away
- Octopuses can change the colour of their skin to match their surroundings so that they can hide in plain sight

- Octopuses have 3 hearts and blue blood
- Octopuses are thought to have been the first intelligent creatures on Earth
- One particular type of octopus, the Blue-Ringed octopus, is known to be one of the most venomous sea creatures in the world

O

Oh Octopus, oh so ever clever,

Eight arms, no bones whatsoever,

Swimming and walking beneath the sea,

But flying, no, you'd never be!

Platypus
Did you know?

- There is only one type (species) of platypus in the world
- Platypuses live in Australia and Tasmania

- Platypuses are one of the most unusual creatures in the animal kingdom – they have a bill like a duck, a tail like a beaver's, fur like an otter's and webbed feet
- When the first ever platypus was seen in England, people didn't believe it was a real animal because it was so odd-looking

- Platypuses are one of only 5 mammals that lay eggs instead of having babies (mammals normally have babies)
- Female platypuses produce milk for their babies like sweat and their babies drink it from their fur

- Platypus's bills are so sensitive that they look for food underwater with their eyes, nose and ears closed and just use their bills to find food
- Platypuses store their food in their cheeks underwater until they can swim back up to eat it

- Platypuses are excellent swimmers underwater but need to come up for air every minute or so
- Platypuses don't have teeth, and use gravel to help them "chew" their food

- Platypuses don't have stomachs
- Platypuses store half of their body fat in their tails and use it for food in emergency times when they don't have any other food to eat

P

The deep blue sky was heard to sigh

"How odd you are, oh my, oh my!"

Said the platypus, tongue-in-cheek

"I'm not odd. I'm unique!"

Quetzal

Did you know?

- There are 6 different types (species) of quetzal in the world
- Quetzals are medium-sized, very brightly-coloured birds found mainly in the tropical rainforests of Central and South America

- Quetzals are thought to possibly be the world's most beautiful birds
- You can recognise quetzals by their bright red, green and blue plumage and very long tail feathers

- Female quetzals are not as brightly coloured as the males
- In male quetzals, the tail feathers can grow up to 3 feet long

- It takes about 3 years for the male quetzal's tail feathers to grow so long
- Quetzals love to live in high, moist, cool areas with lots and lots of trees and bushes, like cloud forests

- Quetzals make their homes in holes high up in trees which they've either built themselves or have been abandoned by woodpeckers
- Quetzals have 2 toes facing forward and 2 facing backwards on each foot to make it easier for them to perch high up on trees

- Quetzals are rarely seen on the ground because the way their feet are makes it hard for them to walk
- Quetzals mostly call during misty times at dusk and dawn but rarely call during very sunny or windy days

- Guatemala's currency is named after the quetzal in honour of the bird
- One particular species, the Resplendent quetzal, was considered to be sacred by the ancient Mayan and Aztec civilisations

Q

The swaying tree smiled in delight

At the beautiful bird high in flight

"Come friend, Quetzal, rest your wings

Good to see you, how are things?"

Rhino

Did you know?

- There are 5 different types (species) of rhino in the world – White, Black, Indian, Javan and Sumatran
- White and Black rhinos live in Africa and the rest in Asia

- White rhinos are the second largest land animal, after the elephant
- White and Black rhinos are both grey in colour

- Rhinos are known for the horns that grow from their snouts; Indian and Javan rhinos have 1 horn and the others have 2
- Rhino horns are made of keratin, the same stuff that people's hair and nails are made of

- Rhino babies (calves) are born without horns but will start to grow them within a few months
- Rhino horns continue growing for the rhino's lifetime, and if one falls off a new one will grow back

- Rhinos have extremely thick, tough skin which is like armour, but they are still sensitive to sunburn and insect bites
- When it gets hot rhinos like to relax in muddy pools – the mud protects their thick skin from the sun like a natural sunblock

- Rhinos are often seen with little birds on their backs, called oxpeckers, who feed on the ticks and insects on the rhinos' backs
- Rhinos have a great sense of smell and hearing but very poor eyesight

- Rhinos communicate with each other through their very smelly poos; the poo smell is unique to each rhino and gives them information about each other
- White rhinos all head to the same place, called a midden, to poo

R

"Rhino, rhino, were you born

With that truly splendid horn?"

"No, no, friend, it grew from hair

When I'm charging best beware!"

Seahorse

Did you know?

- There are thought to be between 45 and 54 different types (species) of seahorse, found in saltwater oceans and seas throughout the world
- Seahorses belong to a group of fish known as bony fish

- Seahorses can range in size from about half an inch to about 14 inches
- Seahorses don't have scales like other fish; they have a skeleton on the outside instead

- Seahorses don't have any teeth or a stomach so food passes straight through them and they have to eat almost constantly to stay alive
- Seahorses swim upright and are actually quite bad swimmers; they are among the slowest swimmers in the ocean and can get very tired very quickly

- The slowest-moving fish in the world is the dwarf seahorse
- Seahorses travel faster hanging onto floating seaweed than by swimming

- Seahorses use their flexible tails to hang on to seaweed and coral to rest, sometimes for days at a time
- Seahorses can move up, down, forward and backward

- Seahorses have great eyesight; one eye can look forward at the same time as the other looks backward
- Seahorses can change their colour to match their surroundings so that they can hide in plain sight

- Seahorses have a small crown on their head which is unique in shape and colour to each seahorse
- Seahorses are only one of 3 creatures in the world where the male gets pregnant and has babies (pipefish and sea dragons are the other 2)

S

The swirling sea was heard to say

"Munch, munch, munch I hear all day

The seahorse eats without a break

All the food that he can take!"

Tortoise

Did you know?

- There are thought to be between 40 and 50 different types (species) of tortoise in the world
- Tortoises have been around for more than 200 million years

- Tortoises are the longest living land animals and can live for a very long time, some as long as 150 years
- Tortoises have a skeleton on the outside and on the inside

- Tortoise shells are made up of 60 different bones joined to one another and are sensitive to the touch so can feel every rub, pet or scratch
- Even though tortoises are known for walking very slowly, they can travel up to 4 miles in one day

- Tortoises can't swim and only live on land
- Tortoises are cold-blooded animals and need to spend time in the sun to keep warm

- Tortoises smell using the roof of their mouth
- Tortoises don't have teeth, they have strong mouths and ridges to mash their food

- Tortoises have to empty their lungs before they go into their shell
- Tortoises starve themselves to empty their stomachs before hibernating in the winter

- Tortoises have special muscles to help them breathe because their hard shells stop their chests from puffing out when they breathe
- Tortoises can hold their breath for long periods of time
- In 1968, 2 tortoises were sent into space where they circled the Moon before arriving back on Earth alive and well

T

"Slow and steady is my pace

As I go from place to place."

"Well, Sir Tortoise, please go slow

We won't rush you as you go!"

Umbrellabird

Did you know?

- There are 3 different types (species) of umbrellabird in the world
- Umbrellabirds are unusual-looking birds found in the tropical rainforests of Central and South America

- Umbrellabirds are about the same size as crows and almost entirely black except one type (species) which has a red patch on its chest
- Umbrellabirds have a unique feature of feathers on the tops of their heads which face forward, called a crest, which can spread out to look like an umbrella

- Umbrellabirds have an inflatable pouch hanging from their throats, called a wattle, which they use to make very loud noises
- Each species has a different kind and size of wattle and in one particular species it can grow as long as 14 inches

- Umbrellabirds spend almost all of their day perched in the tops of tall trees, keeping very still and quiet for long periods
- Umbrellabirds are not very good at flying and prefer to hop from branch to branch rather than fly

- When umbrellabirds do fly, they are slow and clumsy in the air and can only fly short distances
- Umbrellabirds build their nests really high up inside trees

- Only the female umbrellabird builds the nest
- Umbrellabirds don't migrate across land, they migrate up and down mountains

U

Umbrellabird, high in its nest

Like a crow, but with a crest

See that brolly on its head!

Morning, night and going to bed!

Vole

Did you know?

- There are about 155 different types (species) of vole in the world
- Voles look like mice (and are often called field or meadow mice) but their tails are shorter and their ears are smaller

- Voles can live in many different types of habitats ranging from forests to meadows to swamps to grasslands
- Voles have different-coloured fur depending on where they live

- Voles like to live in colonies and any one colony can have up to 300 voles living in it
- Most vole types (species) live in underground burrows but some species live in trees

- Voles are expert tunnel makers and burrow underground to look for plant roots and bulbs to eat
- Gardeners don't like voles because voles dig tunnels under their gardens which damage the grass, plants and trees

- Voles are very good eaters; they can eat almost their own weight in food every day
- Voles can be excellent swimmers and divers

- Voles can run very fast, up to 6mph
- Some smaller species of vole only live between 2 and 6 months but larger species can live 2 to 3 years

- Voles can have babies 5 to 10 times a year and can have 3 to 6 babies at a time
- Voles don't hibernate

V

Sweet little vole, seen as such a pest

Small and cute but never a guest

You're shooed away without a care

"Don't dig here. Don't you dare!"

Wolf

Did you know?

- There are 3 different types (species) of the wolf in the world – Grey, Red and Ethiopian
- Wolves live together in groups called packs and each pack has one leader which the others follow
- Wolves form very strong relationships and family bonds, and wolf couples will usually stay together for life
- The whole pack helps to raise and take care of all the wolf cubs in their pack
- Wolves howl for many reasons such as to warn rival packs to keep away or to contact a separated member of the pack or to call the pack together
- A wolf howl only lasts for about 3 to 7 seconds but seems much longer when many wolves howl together
- A wolf howl can be heard up to 6 miles away
- Wolves can run up to 35mph for short periods but can trot at about 7 to 10mph all day
- Wolves run on their toes which means they can stop and turn easily
- Wolves' jaws are massive and so powerful they can crush bones in just a few bites
- Wolves can smell you from over a mile away
- Wolves can hear from 6 miles away
- Wolves have webbed paws and can swim up to 8 miles at a time
- A wolf cub's eyes are blue at birth but change to yellow-gold between 8 and 16 weeks
- Unlike other animals, wolves communicate with each other through clear (distinctive) facial expressions
- Wolves will respond to people howling

W

Howling in the forest black

The wolf warns off the other pack

"Stay away! Don't come here!

I'm telling you! Keep well clear!"

Xerus

Did you know?

- There are 4 different types (species) of xerus in the world
- Xeruses only live in Africa

- Xeruses are quite large squirrels with short bristly light or dark brown fur and a white stripe running down each side (except one species which doesn't have a stripe)
- Xeruses have a very bushy tail which is almost as big as their body

- Xeruses are also known as the African ground squirrel
- Some species of xerus like to live together in groups but other species like to live alone or in pairs

- Male xeruses like to form their own groups, called bands, which can have about 19 or 20 animals
- Xeruses live in burrows in different types of habitats such as woodlands, grasslands and savannahs

- Xeruses spend a lot of time socialising, sunbathing, or looking for and storing food
- On really hot days, xeruses will lie with their bellies against stones or sand to cool down, or return to their burrows to get away from the heat

- When eating, xeruses sit straight up so they can run quickly if they feel threatened in any way
- Xeruses greet each other by sniffing nose-to-nose

- Xeruses don't hibernate
- Xeruses are often kept as pets and behave similarly to pet cats

X

In a land a plane ride away

Is where I live and spend my day

I'm a Xerus, small and sweet

Sniffing noses when I greet!

Yak
Did you know?

- There are thought to be 2 different types (species) of yak in the world – domestic and wild
- Most yaks are domestic; there are very few wild yaks left

- Domestic and wild yaks look different - wild yaks are larger and have longer fur
- Yaks live in the Himalayan mountains and are the highest living mammals in the world

- Yaks can live that high because they have very big lungs to help them breathe in lots of oxygen
- Yaks can live in extremely cold weather and survive temperatures as low as -40 degrees C with their long thick woolly hair and short fur underneath to keep them warm

- Yaks will get too hot and unwell (heat exhaustion) if the temperature is above about 15 degrees C
- Yaks are often seen bathing in cold lakes and rivers, even in freezing temperatures

- At night or in snowstorms yaks huddle up together, with the young yaks (calves) in the middle
- Yaks grunt, not moo like cows

- Yaks have horns on each side of their head, and in males these can grow as big as about 40 inches long
- Yaks like to live in herds, and though a herd can have hundreds of yaks it is usually much smaller
- Hair from a yak's tail is used to make fake beards for actors in Chinese opera

Y

The snowy mountain stretched and yawned

A brand new day smiled and dawned

The yaks up on the mountain high

Beamed "Good morning, Earth and Sky."

Zebra

Did you know?

- There are thought to be 3 different types (species) of zebra in the world – plains, mountain and Grevy's
- Zebras belong to the same family as horses and donkeys

- Zebras make similar sounds to a horse's snort and a donkey's bray but have a high-pitched bark too
- Each zebra has a unique pattern of black and white stripes and no 2 zebras have the same pattern

- The skin of a zebra is actually black
- Zebra babies, called foals, recognise their mothers by the pattern of her stripes as well as by her smell and call

- A mother zebra will keep her new foal away from other zebras for 2 or 3 days until the foal can recognise her stripes, smell and call
- Zebras can run very fast, reaching speeds of up to 65mph

- Foals can run along with the herd within a few hours of being born
- Zebras run from side to side in a zigzag pattern when being chased

- Zebras sleep standing up
- Zebras have an extremely strong kick and have been known to kick other zebras to death

- Zebras have a very vicious bite and will bite people if they come too close
- Zebras are social animals and live in small family groups within larger herds

Z

"Black, white stripes look good on you

Beautiful and striking too

I see you, Zebra, in the crowd

So unique, and rather loud!"

Every effort has been made to ensure the facts about each animal contained in this book are accurate and correct at the time of publication.

The publisher and author take no responsibility, and disclaim any liability, concerning any inaccuracies.

No part of this book may be reproduced or stored in a retrieval system or transmitted in any form or by any means, electronic, mechanical, photocopying, recording or otherwise without the express written permission of the author and/or publisher.

Text copyright © Sunita Mckenzie (S.P. Aggy), 2022

Illustration copyright © Lakshmi Skala, 2022

All rights reserved

ISBN-13 9798750473168

Printed in Great Britain
by Amazon